CLAW MARKS ON THE BATHROOM FLOOR

SHREYA CHUGH

Made with ♥ on the Notion Press Platform
www.notionpress.com

This book is dedicated to Me, for I deserve a happy ending of my own.

Contents

Contents

About The Author

Shreya Chugh is a poet who considers her words as a mirror to her soul, using poetry as a deeply personal form of self-expression. For Shreya, poetry is a means to converse with herself, a therapeutic outlet for navigating the challenges of living through depression. Through her work, she captures experiences and emotions that often defy spoken words, finding solace and strength in verse.

A published poet with chapters in multiple anthologies, Shreya is currently the Content Head of Nibs & Brushes, the Literature & Fine Arts Society at Aryabhatta College, University of Delhi. Her leadership journey began as Secretary of the Editorial Board at Delhi Public School, Ranipur, and she has since won numerous writing competitions at various levels. Her

Instagram poetry blog, now six years strong, is both a chronicle of her growth as a writer and a platform for sharing her voice with readers.A student of Psychology at the University of Delhi, Shreya combines her academic insights and personal experiences as a neurodivergent individual to bring authenticity and depth to her writing. When not writing, she can be found immersed in books, painting, or music—continually drawing inspiration from the arts and the world around her.

Check her out : @_scintillating_shreya on Instagram

Foreword

It is with immense pride and joy that I write this foreword for **Clawmarks on The Bathroom Floor**, a collection of poetry by one of our very own students, Shreya Chugh. As the principal of Aryabhatta College, University of Delhi, I have had the privilege of witnessing the talent and creativity that Shreya brings to the art of poetry.

Claw Marks on the bathroom floor is a compilation of autobiographical poems, inspired by the author's own life. These poems span through topics like mental health, adolescence, and life through the eyes of a girl in India.

Despite being a co - author to a number of anthologies, this is Shreya's first completely self written book, written in hopes that teens like her find some peace in knowing that they are not alone in navigating through this chaotic world.

Evolving through months of editing and writing, this book is the result of a number of sleepless nights and a lot of hard work, as Shreya's debut into the world of published authors!

I wish Shreya all the best for her future, and I hope that she keeps writing for years to come and keeps us just as proud as she has made us today !

Prof. Manoj Sinha, Principal, Aryabhatta College,
University of Delhi

Acknowledgements

It has taken me years to finally sit and write my verses into a book and this one's for all those people who kept believing in my ability to do it. The very first thank you to Mumma for my poetry starts and ends with you and Papa, for unconditional love and faith , this book exists because you both do.

And to the Almighty God and the Universe, for an incredible life and an even better destiny.

The biggest of my thanks to Pihu Srivastava, for an absolutely incredible front cover, I am yet to meet an artist as adept as you are and to Animesh Dabral for his help with the graphics, you are an absolute life-savior.

To Prakriti, Simran, Priya, Jhanvi and Ayush, my siblings in this life and forever more, thank you, for loving me and for teaching me what it meant to be alive.

To Dr. Richa Arya, for being incredibly kind with my words and my soul and to Ma'am Neena Makkar, Ma'am Rachna Yadav and Krish Sir, for believing in my writing and for trusting me with the English language, the halls of DPS Ranipur shined with your presence.

Thank You, to Paridhi, Raj, Drishti and Lavanya, because you guys let me write, even on days it is raw and wild, you still read it and on days I am raw and wild, you still love me and to Shreya, Ananya, Vyansh, Tanvi and Ajitesh for you guys stay constant reminders of love and support in this life of mine, and to Zohaib, my writer in crime since forever and forever.

I have had the priviledge of getting to know a number of absolutely incredible people, a family, as teachers and as friends, my absolute gratitude to all of them, for they have left their marks on me, and those marks shall never fade.

Finally, to all those who brought me pain ; thank you for breaking my heart, I needed it for my content.

And to you, dear reader, for picking this book up and honouring me with your interest in reading .

Thank You.

2025, Winter Edition

Dehradun, UK

1.*

THE ~~HOME~~TOWN CHAPTER

THE CHILDHOOD I'VE LOST

I find myself mourning quite a lot these days,

Mourning the loss of all the joyful times I've had...

I don't know if I was happy back then,

But I'm sure I wasn't this sad..

I find myself drawing parallels,

Comparing my life across the decades I've been alive...

And each time I reach the same conclusions,

That maybe,

Maybe I should have held on to that innocence aged five...

That Maybe I should have closed my eyes,

When they hugged those other kids...

Maybe I should have shut my ears,

When I cried and they batted no eyelids...

Maybe I should have taped <u>my</u> mouth shut,

When the first sob tore out from my throat...

Maybe I should have seen it coming,

When my first rights to love were revoked...

So, If I hadn't strayed past that tender age of five,

Would I have been any better?

If I had remained a loveable toddler,

Maybe my marks and weight wouldn't have mattered...

And if I hadn't gotten a single scar,

Would they have called me impressive?

If I was a child so full of love,

Would they have still labelled me obsessive?

I find myself unanswerable,

There's nowhere to call home...

Is there a chance for me to smile?

Or just like the fallen time,

Has it also gone?

I've been wishing for those days to come back again,

I find myself willing to pay the cost...

It's been a decade and I find myself still mourning,

Mourning the shine that my eyes once had,

Mourning the loss of the childhood that I lost...

PAPER TOWN

Driving through the roads of this place I've called my "home" town, I realise there's no place that feels like home anymore. Looking for a place to stop and breathe in, I realise that no houses really welcome me, it's a slow epiphany, it creeps through my feet and slowly spreads everywhere until I'm reeling with the loss and the pain of it all, until I'm too breathless to drive. But I still push on in hopes that finally I'll come across a corner which will not ripple like a painful echo in my head, and I drive till the fuel in my Activa is alarmingly low, and yet no matter how far I go, there's no place, no person, no memory to call home. So what do I call this town now? Do you still call a hometown, a hometown even when it's anything but a home?

HOME

What if home was never a person or a place, what if home was a time, a time that would never ever come back again. What if home was the night we stayed up talking till 3 AM, what if home was the evening we held the house party for the first time, what if home was the day you held my hand for the first time, what if home was the week I spent in a resort when I was 12, what if home was the moment I woke up to your texts, what if home was every single second before the epiphany that I never was home. And I don't know where, what or whom to call home anymore, you took away the time, the place and yourself when you left, and now I have no more nouns to go to, all I'm left with is a thousand What Ifs. What if home stopped existing the day we did, what if home itself was a lie just like we were, what if I'd never find home again, what if I never knew what home was, what if I never had a home, what if home does not exist?

2. **

THE FIRST ~~LOVE~~ CHAPTER

LOVE YOU MORE

I want to write you a poem,

Or a journal maybe...

I want to sing you songs,

And let you crave me...

I want to write you letters,

But I'm locking them in a box...

I want you to find the keys,

But I've hidden away the lock...

I want you to know what I think,

But I bury those thoughts away...

I want to tell you a thousand things,

All the details of my days...

There's a battle going on,

My heart's the battlefield...

The devil on my shoulder whispering nothings,

But the angels said that you love me...

Who shall I listen to?

How shall I pick apart the false from the truth?

I'm scared to listen to both the sides,

The devil was once an angel too...

So I'm backspacing my sentences,

I'm holding off my words...

I'm scared that in the game of love,

I'll come third...

What shall I do?

When my heart falls into a mess?

I've been thinking only of you,

And of your warm caress...

But I don't know how to say it,

How to tell you in words...

I hope you just string them together,

Make sense of all you heard...

Because there's only so much words,

That I can hold in my pen,

So now that I'm writing this poem down,

Are we even?

I've given away parts of me,

To people who didn't deserve it...

I've been told to stop loving,

I had once curbed it...

But I want to love you without fears,

To let myself fall...

Can you please be the one to catch me?

(Also, why are you so tall?)

I'll let you into my heart I promise,

Can you try knocking at my door?

I've been afraid for so long babe,

This time, finally,

Can I love you more?

HOLD ME CLOSE

I find myself questioning,

How did we mess things up again?

Out of all the emotions created,

How do we manage to end up with pain?

And there's nothing to be done,

This time too we're both terribly apart...

In hurting us more than I thought it could,

Distance has played it's perfect part...

I find myself helpless,

As all that unshed pain keeps pouring...

I clutch my teddy bear close,

The storm inside me's roaring...

Through all those days we've spent away,

The distance has become more painful slowly...

Your absence was always predetermined,

But these days have become increasingly lonely...

My hand feels alone,

Not holding you feels wrong...

How do I sit here and wait,

I'm, I'm not that strong...

So tell me what shall we do now?

What will happen if I run back home...

Everyday without you seems like a decade,

In this much time, they managed to build Rome...

So can you take my hand?

When you see me again?

Can you hold me tight,

Let go of our pain?

It's been so long,

The God of fates has been cruel...

I've been hurting for a while now,

Been challenging the Gods to a duel..

So I'm writing this as a letter,

Keep it close to your soul...

I've been half a heart without you,

Can you find me and make me whole...

The road taken this time is a harsh one,

On the brink of death, it's the option we chose...

I've been having a hard time babe,

So when we meet again,

Can you hold me close?

ADORABLE

I tell him he is adorable,
I tell him that I adore him
Each time I want to say "I love you".,
I say " You're adorable "...

Because I am scared to say the L word,
Scared that the day I'll say it,
He'd leave...

Scared that he'd become common,
That I'd have to say " Other people"
When I'd talk of him...

And I realise that I stopped using the word, " Love",
I stopped saying I love you(s) to people,
Because I'm scared...

Scared because boys leave,
That they leave when they get to know that they're important to me...
Scared that all I am is just a game,
And my love is just a level that they wish to crack...
Scared that I'm just a competition,
And my love is just a trophy they wish they have...
And I get scared,
Scared when they tell me that they can read me like a book,
Because they'll finish reading and leave me on the shelf....

I continue settle for "I adore you",
I settle in hopes that someday,
Someday he would search up the word " Adore"
That he would find "love" In the synonyms...
That he would look me in the eyes,
And would know my reasons...
And then maybe, when he will tell me that he loves me,
I will say it back..

But if that day never comes,
If he leaves before I can promise my love...
I'll go back to adore and hold it close...

And I'll wait on the balcony of my lonely castle,
For another boy with love...
And I'll wait with my broken heart,
For another boy with glue...

3. ***

THE ~~FIRST~~ HEARTBREAK CHAPTER

THE SOULMATE OF RAIN

I was soulmates with Rain,

I loved listening when it talked...

And everytime it came by,

The chaos around me stopped...

Rain felt like a hug,

To my touch starved skin...

And it treated me with love,

I was it's own kin...

It was magical, rain, I mean..

But all boons come with a bane,

In the river of happiness,

There shall always be pain...

And such was my curse,

I had no ways to hide...

I was meant to make a choice,

Forced to pick a side...

And when I didn't make a move,

The destiny chose for me..

In the choice between the rain & the sun,

Rain was meant to be...

No matter what was to be done,

I couldn't have had them both...

The choice was meant to be made,

I could no longer trod on two roads...

Thus a lesson was learnt,

Those tapestries of the future came undone...

In the wars of water and fire,

I wasn't meant to love the sun...

So here I am, a soulmate of rain,

Walking away from the fire...

Giving up on my patrons,

My heart isn't up for hire..

After all my battles, came that war,

A story written of tears and pain...

The story of that girl,

Who had to give up her love for the sun,

The story of that soulmate of rain...

SCRATCHES

I've been showering three times a day,

In hopes that your prints will finally wash off,

I've been going out in every rain, trying to remove marks of you.

I sit, trying to drown, trying to scrub your memories away,

Tears pour and dry out, so do the screams, but your prints stay.

And I scrub my skin, desperately scratching off your traces,

Until my skin's red and my nails have drawn out blood,

Yet you don't disappear,

And I tiredly slump down on the floor,

In hopes that I'll succeed in washing myself off you the next time,

And yet again as I step into the shower, the traces are still there,

The reminders of the betrayal.

CARVING A DAGGER

From my heart of gold,

I broke off A piece...

Put it on a furnace,

And bought it to heat...

Watched in pain,

As it melted away...

And hoped that it would be enough,

To make you stay...

I took that gold,

And carved A knife out of it...

Carved all my pain,

And kept carving till I deemed fit..

I took your hand in mine,

And handed you the dagger...

Too euphoric are being yours,

I didn't see you hiding her...

I let my guards down,

And behind me you stood still...

And with my dagger in your hand,

You went in for the kill...

Bleeding from your wound,

I looked you in the eye...

Too used to this pain,

This time, I couldn't even cry...

And I walked off forever,

Put our story away..

You might have preyed on me,

But I wasn't the prey...

So keep that dagger,

You can have it...

You might have left a scar,

But it missed my heart by a bit...

I'm still alive,

I’m still breathing...

And you’re just a footnote,

In my life’s screening...

I'm closing the book now,

Putting an end to your matter...

The weapon is yours to keep,

There’s your name on the dagger...

MINE

"Mine" is a controversial word, it's there, it means something, but it's unexplainably impossible. Nothing can be mine, you're not mine to have, they weren't mine to be, this place isn't mine to call home, nothing's mine and it'll never be. But at the same time, as unfair as it may seem, I had been "yours", I had been "Theirs", I had belonged to this place. I had always been " Someone's", "Somewhere's", I had always been there, securely, like a home that would never go anywhere until you picked up a hammer and slowly, piece by piece, you broke me down. You were unfair, they were unfair, this town was unfair, because all of you stole me away from myself, because you all made me yours and yet none of you were mine to have, and yet none of you were mine to love.

WE WEREN'T LOVE

Love doesn't take your breathe away,

It doesn't give you anxiety...

It doesn't make you jealous,

It doesn't fire your insecurity...

What we had was never love,

It was a social media brand at most...

I was happy in my denial,

And you were using me to open doors...

I was your wingwoman,

Jealousy works well with girls...

And you were my hallucination,

Until the story completely unfurled...

I kept your thoughts close,

They were a fake reassurance...

Social reputation was at stake,

And we were fixing it with the dance...

I was your first score,

Your pure and dumb fantasy...

But we were never what I wished for,

Rather a curse that bound me...

So we kept dancing,

Till we were out of breath...

And you chose to lie,

While I unleashed my wrath...

You weren't my rom com,

You were my tragedy...

A story of blood & tears,

One of infidelity...

We were painfully beautiful,

Beautiful while we lasted...

Yet there was nothing beautiful about us,

We were a war already forecasted...

In the era of phones and connection,

We'd choose to be silent...

What I had thought of as a home,

Was just plain violence...

You were ethereal,

And so incredibly persistent...

And you had blood on your hands,

The bane of my existence...

We were a bloodbath,

Backstabbing gossip when push came to shove...

I have a thousand adjectives for whatever we were,

We were a lot of things,

But we weren't love...

P.S.

Not all love stories are beautiful, and most of them are not even love. It takes a long time to realise what love is, and an even longer span to move over the fact that what you had was never really love. This is a piece about how "love" Is generally a bloodbath masked with a cutesy concept, it's generally a fistfight, it's life or death and those that make it out alive have to live with the consequences of their choices and blood on their hands for the rest of their lives.

TRIGGER WARNINGS

Blood & Gore never hurt me,

But your reminders do...

When you randomly appear,

In an Instagram post or two...

My perfectly okay heart,

Breaks a little again...

You course through me,

Like a silver of pain...

You flash like a thousand memories,

A hail storm on my heart...

I feel my throat tighten,

And breathing becomes hard...

After spending a lifetime,

Having panic attacks in your arms...

You yourself are my trigger,

The one bringing me harm...

You appear like a sudden hail storm,

The knife in my stomach twists again...

After a thousand years without you,

The wound when prodded hurts the same...

And I find myself afraid,

Of my own damn phone...

Of the colors of your jacket,

Of the smell of your cologne...

I freeze on the side walk,

When I see someone in the French flag...

When someone takes your name,

And my entire system lags...

And when you're mentioned on stories,

Of people I once called friends...

I get nightmares of you,

Of you holding her hands...

I feel my entire body shut down,

And the room temperature hits a 100° figure...

It passes after a second,

Leaving the memories that you triggered...

And how I wish for some peace,

For a city where we didn't happen...

For a place where my heart would be full,

And my eyes would be laughing...

But unfortunately for me,

You're a stain in my past...

One that our friends don't let me forget,

The kind that lasts...

Oh how I prayed,

For our them to forget our glories...

To know that I'll get hurt,

And hide their stories...

I don't know what to do,

Five months and I still find myself mourning...

If they were going to post you after all,

You could have at least come with a trigger warning.

4. ****

THE MOVING ~~ON~~ CHAPTER

WORTH NO NIGHTMARES

I woke up again today,

Streaks of a fading nightmare in my head...

And at last yet again,

I didn't dream of you...

Years of torture and pain,

Years that I have been bearing in vain...

They have healed me up slowly,

And your horrifying memory is fading away...

First you lost your place in this life of mine,

And then you eventually lost my respect...

At last, my life's coming full circle,

And your name has no meaning left...

Looks like my demons are forgetting you too,

Feels like an answer to my prayers...

And after all your betrayals years back,

At last, you're not even worth my nightmares...

I have borne scars on my skin,

For the entirety of this life...

The one you <u>gave shall fade away</u> too,

Your love wasn't worth the price of your knife...

Looks like you couldn't kill me after all,

And I yet again came back stronger...

I'll find hundreds of you out there,

But no kingdom shall I not conquer...

No words are left to say,

Two years and my thirst of closure has faded away...

You and me don't even stand on the same ground today,

I have no thoughts of-what it could have been...

"And today I'm living in a big old city,

And all you still are is mean..."

People like you deserve no screen time,

In this movie that my psyche builds...

And the only thing your memories deserved,

Was letting them get brutally killed...

Watch me rise again today,

Holding close, my battle scars and tears...

Look at yourself in the mirror again,

You're worth no nightmares...

MAKING SPACE

I wake up to my phone screaming,

It has out of space(s)...

In my overflowing tub of memories,

There wasn't place for new faces...

So I sit and start to sort,

Removing memories hold no more weight...

This messed up way of my life,

I am finally setting straight...

From my too full life,

I'm removing traces of you...

From that darkness you gifted me,

I'm finall breaking through...

It's been too much,

I have housed you inside me for a long time,

My home deserves a better tenant,

Than someone committing metaphorical crimes..

Your existence shall mean nothing more to me,

You don't deserve a single byte...

You may have thought you were winning,

But I am victorious in our fight...

So. I sit here cleaning,

Freaking both me and my phone...

I'm going back to our path,

Un-turning each stone..

So that the new ones can come in,

New memories can be clicked...

And this too broken story,

can finally be fixed...

I'm telling you it's over,

The high wasn't worth the pain...

I don't want to handle you anymore,

So I'm putting an end to our refrain...

After turning away from your lies,

I find my self with a blank place...

And to let new people in,

I finally have enough space...

And this time I'll name my heart,

To someone who deserves it...

That folder of your name disappears,

And I'm left with a clean chit...

I've known you were talking shit

This time I'll let life hit you back with that phrase...

I'm hope you can get out now,

My soul's knocking on my door,

She's glad that I'm finally making space....

YOU SHALL HEAL

There's shards,

Stabbed onto your back...

There's cracks,

On that heart of glass...

But keep breathing this time,

Keep breathing for me...

Slowly this pain will go away some day,

And you shall heal...

The world feels cold,

As if no goodness ever existed here...

There's nothing to be happy for,

Absolutely nothing remains...

But smile a bit more,

Smile for me...

You'll have reasons to be happy someday,

And you shall heal...

You're on the floor again,

Too tired to bear anymore...

The darkness doesn't seem to go away,

There's no light to search for...

But keep hoping this time,

Hope for me...

Your hope will be fulfilled someday,

And you shall heal...

Even on days when it's all wrong,

When your entire existence seems a curse...

And also on days when you're happy,

But there's a dull ache inside your heart...

Try loving yourself forever,

Try loving yourself for me...

You will hold yourself close someday,

And you shall heal..

I know of your pain,

You know of me...

I know of your cries,

I have felt what you feel...

And some day,

When it rains, when it's sunny...

When it's sour, when it's honey...

The universe will shift a bit,

And you shall heal...

5. *****

THE ~~FRIEND~~SHIP CHAPTER

BIRTHDAYS & PARTIES

My birthdays and parties don't mix,

Friends and lovers and extremely long bills...

Weeks spent planning,

And yet again each time it goes down hill...

Those gatherings with friends,

Friends that became strangers too quick...

The videos I took that day,

Now just make me feel sick...

I should have stayed home,

Blood's always thicker than watered down covers...

Birthdays were to be spent with family,

Not with backstabbing acquaintances and cheating lovers...

Because each time I throw a party,

I lose the people I invite...

Because each time I call up friends,

We break up in issues of pride...

I was correct when I said,

That I shouldn't throw a bash...

Why waste money,

On relationships which didn't last?

Because you weren't deserving,

You weren't worth it...

The heart break was painful,

And I was pushed to the edge of it...

I deserved better that you,

Better than friends who cut me off,

Better than lovers who call it off,

Better than brothers who're there for the name,

Better than dates just had for fame...

I should have been loved,

Treated like the queen I am...

I should have had a loyal birthday,

Instead of a sparkling mayhem...

It wasn't a teenage Dream,

If I was the third wheel there...

It wasn't the birthday I hoped for,

When I spend the night thinking if you cared...

Because you made me sad,

And I had to fake a smile...

Because in my own birthday,

I wasn't in the limelight...

I spent the entire night,

Asking you if you were okay...

After I had to beg you,

To be present on my favorite day...

I had a great time,

Ill confess to the guilty pleasure...

But if I had known it would be worth nothing,

I would have spent the day in leisure....

Because you weren't worth,

The hard work my mom dad lent...

Because you weren't worth,

The money they had to spend...

So now that the year's done and dusted,

Now that I'll never see your faces again...

I hope I'll never have friends like you,

That my parade never gets rained...

Because that crowd of twenty,

That I loved from the very start...

Because that crowd of 15,

That broke my very heart...

Because no oaths lasted,

No oaths taken on the river styx...

Because no matter how many years pass,

My birthdays and parties don't really mix...

UP IN SMOKES

We were a happy family,

With those forever dreams...

Finally true friends,

And we were all seen...

And then the games began,

The lovely laughs turned fake...

And the bonds we were proud of,

Slowly faded away...

The last betrayal of school life,

The last set of friends lost...

Lost were the days of those parties,

When I had played host...

Best friends fell apart,

Lovers fell to pieces...

Our once golden sheet,

Had irreversible creases...

And everything changed,

The sparks turned to flames...

And we all slowly,

Became sick of the games...

The heat was the irony,

Of the entire memory...

And we had dug up all the skeletons,

That were once buried...

And that's the thing with fire,

It destroys everything in its path...

And yet it continued to burn bright,

Just like that one fine night in the past...

Those bonds of love & care,

Slowly all broke...

And that beautiful tapestry of us,

Slowly went up in smoke...

I THINK THEY DON'T LIKE ME

The first time I said this out loud I was a kid, it's funny how a kid's not supposed to be that sad but I was and this sentence lives on inside me like a fear. I realised that they didn't like me and I did all I could again and again to make them like me, and then each time I burnt down to the ground, I realised that they still don't. And it's a thing that motivational speakers do where they tell you that you don't need those people who don't want you. But in the play of no man's an island you sit down and wonder if college would be like school, and a little bit of doubt creeps in at their one word replies, and balant ignorance, and my mind asks for the first time in months, "I think they don't like me." And my world ends in seconds behind the eyes that they don't bother to make contact with.

NAMESAKES

It's a boon and a bane,

Having a name so many others have...

The trends of the decade,

With me in its aftermath...

As I was 12 when I realised,

That someone else too has my name...

And all that love and support,

Wasn't my own fame...

I've been living with it in me,

The fear of namesakes...

Those that make me wonder,

If my name was a mistake...

And it's the irony that hurts,

Of how it's always the other one...

How when they say my name,

Its not me who needs to turn...

Because all along this path,

I've met versions of myself...

A factory churning out people my name,

Grabbing my identity of the shelves...

And for years I've lived,

Knowing that my name would call someone else...

That when my name's whispered with love,

It's the others being revered...

I'm at this crossroads again,

Destiny has again played it's part...

Another one with my own name,

A seperate beating heart...

And such was the trap of life,

History repeating itself...

Two stories with the same name,

On a single bookshelf...

But they grab her off the shelf,

As I'm gathering dust...

In this library full of readers,

There are only so many I trust...

With a story like mine,

With innocence(s) aged nine...

With the bloodiest of autobiographies,

In this city of crime...

And someone calls my name,

But it's not for me...

Even my name doesn't come without pain,

In the given and taken of nothing is free...

I know they don't call me,

When psyche(s) come undone...

And each time they ever take my name,

They're always calling the other one...

In people I've found home,

In people I've lost a thousand stakes...

And I write this as my name is called,

Each time referring to my namesakes...

6. ******

THE ~~SECOND~~ LOVE CHAPTER

PARALLEL LINES

He looks like a novel that I've wanted to write for months but no one sees it except me. He's a prickly little porcupine, stinging my bruises and bringing blood out to my skin and he's so beautiful that it hurts to know that I'll never love him. That in the plan of the cosmos, we two weren't written for each other, and he's my parallel line, running besides me, never to be mine and I'm running besides him, never to be his. He's not the kind of guy someone like me can love, his is a love that's supposed to hurt, and open wounds like myself have no business loving men who forget promises immediately after they make them. But he's ethereal and I die a little everytime he breaks into a rare smile, and I find myself praying for the smile to stay forever, but his smiles are built of the hearts he stands on, and I'm a lone life receiving post cards of him knowing that the beauty of his edges will never forgive the fact that he's a war torn land and I'm a soldier too wounded by my own wars to fight his and I know that someday an honoured, uniformed lover would come and he'll break her into a poet and I'm both envious and relieved that it's not going to be me because at the end of it all, he's so perfectly broken that my broken pieces fit his the best but he'll heal and I'll too and we'll fit each other no more and I'm no more the woman who'll break herself for a man again, so I'm passing by, I'll not turn around this time, because if I do and he's looking at me, I'll become his, there'll be nothing of myself left in me and that's a fate that I refuse to accept.

TO LOVE A HEARTBREAKER,

I have a video of him in my gallery that I'll never let anyone see because if I can fall for him that fast then who knows how many more can and I'm scared that he'll fancy a goddess and she'll keep him. He's not mine, he's incredibly annoying, he's a tattoo artist bringing out my blood, he's a lot of things but he's not mine, but this video in my gallery is all I have of him and it's mine and only mine to adore. He makes a writer out of me and he's incredibly ordinary, and I know that but to my love starved heart, he's salvation in flesh and blood and he's more my muse than he's my lover. He leaves me breathless and shaking, he says things so audacious that they make me hate myself for every second that I spend by his side but what is infatuation if not a tragedy and I'm no more than those women in tragedies who were written into the tragedy simply because they loved a man. He has hands so incredibly calloused that I know he has broken enough hearts, but I give him my hand to hold because his seem lonely and men like him shouldn't be lonely. In the irony of all love, my hatred of him and his uncaring smirk runs so deep that he has become a familiar ache in my veins and he's nothing like any of what I've written to the world but to me his eyes look heavy so I cry for him, he talks like a maniac so I shut myself down a bit but most of all it was that video of him smiling, because he smiled like a heartbreaker, so I gave him my heart to break.

THE ABSENCE

Your absence disarms me in a way that the lack of clean air in this city did. It hits me in the face like a cloud of passive smoke from the passerby smokers that I cross each morning and yet no matter how many days pass, it still burns my lungs the same, it still makes my eyes water the same. I haven't loved you for a while now, but the unfortunate things about habits is that they stay even after you stop loving them and I stand on the stage to face the world for the first time in forever but the audience is full of faces I don't know, full of people who I wish I knew but I don't and this epiphany will bleed for a little more of forever because you weren't there, because they weren't there and maybe I've been a little too kind or maybe my anger isn't as justifiable as your pain is but after a lifetime of giving out infinite chances to houses that don't become homes, you still weren't there for me and I still am all on my own.

HOLD HER

I lost you,

Loved you as much as I could...

I was the devastating fire,

To your very flammable woods...

The adult in me is proud,

It seems that she always is...

But the kid in me is still screaming,

Another plan of hers,

I have shattered down to bits...

How do I tell her now?

That what we had wasn't love...

That I wasn't your perfect crime,

And you were not my white dove...

I'll have to live with it,

The blood on my hands...

I've broken my heart again,

Chosen the wrong stance...

I'm fighting her again,

The me aged five...

She fell at your feet too fast,

And now she hates that I'm alive...

You were everything,

A cosmos all at once...

But I watched with a lighter in hand,

As the tapestry of us burned...

Because I couldn't let you read,

All of the stories on her bookshelf...

In wanting to keep her heart safe,

I broke it myself...

And now I have nothing else left,

But pieces of us to pick up...

We were both tearing each other down,

In what we thought was a slight hiccup...

She turned away from me,

Leaving me lonelier that I was...

That never ending euphoria of mine,

Suddenly came to a pause...

And now I'm back here,

In the darkest corners of my heart...

Those demons under both our beds,

Completely tore us apart...

I know you want me no more,

18 year old me,

Again doesn't deserve a shoulder...

But that child has done nothing wrong,

Please protect her from me,

Please hold her...

WRONG PERSON, WRONG TIME

Only if I could have uploaded all our love on a drive, would that have made it more permanent? If your love had a digital footprint I would have encountered your hate with it but you texted out your loathing and kept your love under covers. I saw you and saw a future, and now that it has been taken away from me, I'm once again somehow a home with lights fused, how do I reach this place each time? "It always happens to Shreya", you said and the " Even I'm doing it to her right now." Was silent. "How many times can a heart be mangled and still be expected to keep beating?", my second chance, you were my right person wrong time but I guess the person and time both were wrong, because years of stabs made me the master of knives but you entered the knife fight with a gun and left me bleeding out on the floor. But I'll not bleed into the sun this time, my pain has entertained this world for years now, and it refuses to do so anymore. You came into my life bragging how crying is something you'll never do and I forgot that empty cans are truly empty, the one who never cried could have never loved either and such was my mistake, I tried to make you cry, I tried to make you love but love cannot thaw hearts of ice but ice does spread and lovers freeze, because locking away your heart completely forever, is the only way to preserve it from people like you.

THE CLOSURE

I waited my entire life for you, for someone who caught the words immediately as I breathed them out and wove his own story into them and there you were, in all of your glory, holding out your hand and pulling me up, asking me to dance. But the music swells and ends and you push me down, I let out a scream, one so silent that only you could hear it and I let you walk away. We were perfect, you and I, until we weren't. I still have a video of you in my phone, just that now it looks like a slow motion of how blood baths happen but that's the thing with infatuation, I would hold the bloodied hand because it's yours. We were so much more than we could be and that's as much your tragedy as it's mine and I'll be there tomorrow too, just as much as I am there today and you'll see me laugh under the sun, just to turn around and tell the demon under my bed, how much you hate me. And only if you could be true, only if you could have thought it through. And I'll laugh because I know you are watching, and I'll think to myself like the only morning ritual I could have stuck to. I'll think, "Only if I was laughing for you, laughing would have meant so much more." But I'm not and you're not either and that's where it ends, us two, perfect, too perfect.

7. ******

THE ~~MENTAL~~ ILLNESS CHAPTER

CAGE

I've been holding myself in a cage,

Bars I've put myself behind...

To everyone who's broken me,

I think I've been too kind...

I've let those rebukes hurt me,

I've held my anger in...

For the sake of "peace",

I've let all of them win...

I've been scared for so long,

My fear has begun to suffocate me now...

I think I've forgotten how to love,

The memories in my head are weighing me down...

It's all my doing,

There's no one I can blame...

I'm a burnt kid right now,

'Cause once I too loved the flame...

And I've grown to be afraid of it,

The scars on my skin already hurt enough...

It's hard to breathe in conditions like these,

To breath when you're unbearably stuffed...

But I keep eating more words,

They have now become hard to swallow...

I feel my wind pipe slowly closing over,

My laboured breaths turn more shallow...

All because I've experienced first hand,

The pain those words inflict...

So instead of saying them out loud,

I let them hurt my soul instead...

So that no one else gets hurt,

By my momentary pain...

But all those tries of kindness,

Seem to just go in vain...

The world doesn't hold itself back,

It’s a universe of both love and rage...

As i find myself struggle to breathe,

It’s getting claustrophobic now,

In this very lonely cage...

BROKEN WINGS

"How did this happen?

Weren't we fine just now?

The day every wound healed,

Tore me apart more somehow...

All my hopes by dreams,

Belief that It will finally be okay...

It's all crumbling at my feet,

And I don't remember how to pray...

There's only so much,

That a heart is meant to take...

After a decade of blood and pain,

I thought the heavens owed me a break...

But I am hurting again,

The pain is still as raw as the first time...

And my eighteen year old soul bleeds,

How would it be if I had remained nine...

Because strangers don't become friends,

And houses don't become homes...

They warned me against all vices,

But forgot to warn me against hope...

Days & nights pass,

This life keeps devastating me...

If God gives handleable punishments,

I wonder if he's overestimating me...

I still am a bloodbath,

I have lost too much to keep a score...

And I scream my heart out,

"What was I made for?"

My dreams have turned to dust,

And I'm still reeling with the loss...

There's too much pain at my door...

For me to play host...

And no hands extend in help,

I have angered the Lord of people & things...

I am an angel pushed out of hell,

Bleeding through my broken wings...

I look up at that sky,

Putting my existence up to vote...

That cruel God sheds a tear,

As I sit drenched,

Forever afraid to hope...

PAIN

I've been in pain for far longer than I've been without it, I've breathed and lived my pain, I've woken up screaming and have gone to bed crying. And while I grow up into my ideal life, and on days when my life's great and my demons are silent, that child in me screams apart a storm and leaves me in pain, as if pain is her way of showing she cares, her way of reminding me that she's still there. But every other blue moon, she gets a little too close, too close to that nerve in my neck and I have to sit in the dark and reel with the consequences of her actions. She's my most loyal friend, the lover who never leaves and she smiles at me each time I'm sobbing in my bed, she smiles an "I told you so" and walks away, her footsteps echoing in a room filled with a silence so loud that there's no more space in it for me to whimper.

WHAT CAN I DO FOR YOU

I am tired of my life, whatever little energy I have seeps down into a puddle and I'm tired, I'm standing in a pool of my own pain and the ends of my pants are soaked. And you've been asking me a thousand questions, a hundred hurtful words you've already thrown at me, and I sit at the crossroads of a thousand decisions that a 17 year old shouldn't have to make and you ask me, "What can i do for you?" And my head screams, "Please kill me", " Please keep me alive"," please go back in time and love me more", " Please hold me till I cry my eyes out", "Please let me leave", " Please keep me here", "Please be my home", " This place will never be home" , "Please this" "Please that". And I look at you, and break into a heartbreaking smile, " No, there's nothing I want you to do for me" And I go into my darkness and I cry and I cry and I cry...

THE DRAMA OF MY DREAMS

I'm a life born of drama,

It plays out every day on the stage of my heart...

And all those I've loved or lost,

Play a dramatic part...

There are smiles and tears,

And tears born of a smile...

My brain picks out and puts up the plays,

From it's horrifying pile...

And the drama of my dreams starts,

Rendering me paralyzed from fear...

And from my sleeping consciousness,

Slips down a tear...

This drama has seen some beautiful days,

So immensely beautiful to exist...

And they talk of long lost lovers,

Playing out a moonlit tryst...

And yet as I wake up each day,

I find my life in shambles...

My earth's axis shifted,

And all my hopes trampled...

And I've never known what's worse,

The nightmares on that stage...

Or the ones that I live with,

The ones embedded in my age...

My unconscious bleeds,

Wounds that I refuse to...

And the blood stained you,

Has decided to fuse through...

For every drama I ignore,

There's a nightmare that forms...

The closest of my friends,

Taking nightmarish forms...

All these betrayals,

I live through them again...

My horrific reality,

Bleeds through my pain...

I wonder what Frued would say,

If he interpreted this dream...

Would my pain be validated?

Or is nothing like it seems?

The drama has hit the roof,

And the roof collapsed on me...

The house I built with my hands,

Is completely crumbling...

And The dusk falls into dawn,

The silence rings with my screams....

And every night, all over again,

Starts the drama of my dreams....

8. ********

THE LIFE ~~WELL~~-LIVED CHAPTER

ALL MY LIFE

This isn't how it was supposed to be,

This isn't how it was supposed to be!

I am 12 and I sit rocking back and forth,

Maniacal tears drowning on me...

I struggle and scream,

Kicking and Fighting to be loved somehow...

But no one wanted to play with me when I was 10,

And no one wants to play with me now...

And my inner child screams,

And screams till her voice gives out...

She whispers alone, alone, alone,

Her feathery voice now a silent shout...

I can hear fate laugh in a distance,

Her maniac laughter ringing in my head...

I hear my demons questioning,

Why don't I just die instead...

I finally am going! I and 14 and,

My dreams is here in my hands...

"I'm sorry we can't let you participate"

"Atleast you'll get the certificate"

No you don't understand, no, No, NO, YOU DON'T UNDERSTAND!

No there's no getting better,

It comes back harsher each time...

I have nothing more to give,

I've spent every last dime...

And I'm still trembling,

"I'm scared, I'm scared, I'm SCARED!"

But no one comes to rescue,

And I'm 15 crying in my bus and no one cares...

Spring knocks by and kids are out,

"It's too warm, it's TOO warm, IT HURTS, IT'S TOO WARM!?"

I am an anxious little child,

And even the sun was bringing me harm...

I cannot slip and fall back,

I SCREAM I scream I SCREAM,

I cannot pick up the blade again,

No more smiles feigned...

I was just a kid, I was just a KID, I AM JUST A KID...

Grandma loves her more,

And I run away to my bedroom,

I look into the mirror, I'm 4,

And Grandma loves her more...

And I sit rocking back and forth,

Screams rip out of my throat,

Making it hard to breathe...

"this wasn't how it was supposed to be,

THIS WASN'T HOW IT WAS SUPPOSED TO BE! "

And I'm 8 again,

"It's MY birthday, IT'S MY BIRTHDAY!"

And she wears the dress I loved,

And I cry and I cry and I Cry Away...

I'm 17 and he lies to my face,

"You're lying, you're lying, I KNOW YOU LIED",

The walls around me become a fortress,

And that little girl inside me died...

I see him walk away,

But you're my best friend, YOU'RE MY BEST FRIEND,

He doesn't turn back,

And this piece becomes the bloodiest tale I ever penned...

I'm a child, I'm a pre teen,

I'm a teenager with no dreams...

I wake up from a nightmare,

And I scream, I scream, I scream...

THE LOVERS I NEVER HAD

I was 9 when I sat with with that giggling group of girls,

And when they asked me who I liked, I told them...

Maybe that was the day I lost my purity,

Only if I hadn't loved him, only if I hadn't told them...

And I was still 9 when he came upto me one day,

I was still 9 when his taunts did start...

I was standing terrified of this feeling,

I was nine when my first crush broke my heart...

And suddenly the picture shifted,

I'm 11 and I like my seat partner more than I should...

But he's too good to be true,

And he deserves so much more than I ever could...

I'm 11 and I'm writing him a card,

And I put it in his bag...

I was still eleven when I tore it up,

And told me I had nothing to brag...

I'm 12 when I see him for the first time,

He's beautiful, and I'm on my knees...

I am a naive preteen,

And he's a cherry blossom in the breeze...

I've liked him for three years now,

And he's still as ethereal as a dove...

But his words are now morphing to poison,

It has already made it's way down my neck,

When I realized that my like was now love...

And he pushes me away,

Never once did my best friend look back,

And I was 14 and heartbroken,

I was 14 when I heard my heart crack...

And I remember being 14,

14 and in love with my three year old lie...

And he met me again this time,

All over again to ruin my life...

And he's still loved,

Almost as if he's made of a pile of glitter...

And I'm completely wrecked,

None of us the fitter...

I'm a violin in his arms,

His to guide, his to lose...

And we have no labels,

Just one heart of glass used...

And he broke it again,

The world heard my cries this time...

And I am 15 as I realise,

That all those eagle eyed audience were really blind...

And I hate the concept of love,

I've been broken too much for a doll...

But I'm 16,the world's in love,

And then one fine day I passed him in the hall...

He's incandescent,

And the entire world is on their knees for him,

He walks like his owns this land,

And I'm suddenly a gift for him to keep...

But damn that social anxiety,

In watching him from afar, there's so much joy...

I watched my love fall in love,

And so I found myself another boy...

My boy was chaos,

Ruining both himself and me...

And yet I loved him so much,

Trust me I did...

But we'll not talk of him,

Cause he was my lover indeed...

Who cares if he was there,

For every single damsel in need...

So I turn away, to my never (lover) in the Hall...

But no universes conspired as time passed...

I'm 17 and I wish I was the one he holds,

I wish I was the one sitting by him in class...

And school's over now,

I've broken my heart a thousand times...

I step out of that building still alone,

Bearing scars of A thousand times...

And I watch him walk up to me,

Oh no! Not really, it was me who did...

And I scribble on his shirt,

All the feelings I had hid...

He's 17 and he's ethereal,

My majestic Unrequited love...

And so I poured it in my confession,

Now that push came to shove...

And he doesn't know it was me,

And he shall never guess...

Oh such was my last lover in that building,

He was beautiful

& I was blessed...

And just like those 12 years of school,

I carve this love out on my sketchpad...

And this refrain ends with my schoollife,

The refrain of all the lovers,

I never had...

THE PROTAGONIST

For the longest of my time,

I've wondered what it would take...

For me to become the main character,

And stop being the mistake...

But that's the thing with heroes,

They're carved out of stories...

Blood has to be spilled,

For them to write their glories...

It takes more loss than love,

To make a person into a God...

You have to lose a homeland,

Before you can build an abode...

And such confusion it causes,

The need for tragedy...

Am I worthy of being the hero,

If I still have my sanity?

The question floats in the air,

"Have I managed to lose enough?"

Or am I destined to lose more?

The diamond in the rough...

Would it have been better,

If my unconsciousness came from a war?

And instead of the ever growing anxiety,

A "dementor" tore me apart...

If all that trauma,

Could have shaped me into an icon...

If I had a good enough reason,

For this soul to die for...

And would camp half-blood,

Have been the home I still don't have?

If I had a tragic enough life,

Would my name become the map?

Because it takes fire & tears,

For a hero to be born...

And have I burnt enough,

For my head to be adorned...

There's blood on my hands,

Tears on my cheeks...

Am I finally strong enough,

To not be called weak?

Have I bled enough for you?

Oh my reader, be my catalyst...

Put some respect to my name,

And make me the protagonist...

Dear Reader,

I have put the last seventeen years of my life in this book that you hold in your hands right now, these years were everything and nothing at once, they are the reason I've become who I am today and yet I still cannot figure out if that is a good thing or not. But, however they were, they were mine, and so is this story, and somehow, it is both incredible and unfortunate that it still keeps going, I still keep living and I still find stories that intertwine with mine and become art.

I wrote most of this book on the very bahthroom floor that the title talks about, because it was only there that I was truly in my own company and throughout my life, bathroom floors have been my forever companions, comforting and soothing me with their cold. I had thought that for all of my life, I would only ever find solace on the floor for being on the ground was so much more comforting than the risk of falling was, but as I sit in my warm bed in my big, old city, my life comes full circle. I am telling you this, dear reader, as a reminder, that no matter how cold and hard the ground feels right now, there is a warm bed somewhere, which waits for you to come and dream. So make sure you rest well when it finds you, make sure that your dreams are full of love, the kind of love that makes you feel loved. Make sure, that you love yourself enough to do that.

Thank you dear reader, for picking this book up and treating it with care, you are holding a piece of my heart in your hands; and I am grateful for their warmth.

Yours,

Shreya

www.ingramcontent.com/pod-product-compliance
Lightning Source LLC
LaVergne TN
LVHW091059150826
845673LV00002B/645

* 9 7 9 8 8 9 6 1 0 1 5 2 9 *